A Practical Guide to Financial Success

FINANCE GAME STRONG

Sharang Nadkarni

AUTHOR BIOGRAPHY

Hello reader,

My name is Sharang Nadkarni, and I'm based in San Francisco, California. I'm a fun-living and easy going person, love to travel a lot and experience what life has to offer. During my free time, I love to play sports like tennis, squash, learn new things, reading fiction and non-fiction, writing non-fiction, running, watching good movies and tv shows, Chess, playing the ukulele, practice salsa dancing, exercise and yoga. Most of my time away from work I like to do any activities (Mix of adventure and arts/craft), go hiking, etc.

I like experiencing fun things and FIne adventuRE

activities (pun intended). I am an Investments, Stock market and financial derivatives trading enthusiast, and fond of anything finance related. The idea behind this book is to spread financial literacy and awareness among people of age, race or gender. You can also subscribe to my blog 'nomadnomics.wordpress.com' if you are interested in following my journey and become financially stable and secure. My mission and love for spreading Financial Literacy and help others with wealth building methods, enabled me to write this book.

CONTENTS

Chapter 1 Introduction to Financial Mastery

Chapter 2 Building a Strong Financial Foundation

Chapter 3 Investing Basics Getting Started

Chapter 4 Crafting Your Investment Strategy

Chapter 5 Mastering the Art of Stock Market Investing

Chapter 6 Navigating the Bond Market and Fixed-Income Investments

Chapter 7 Real Estate Investing Generating Passive Income and Building Wealth

Chapter 8 Retirement Planning and Wealth Preservation Chapter 9 Tax-Efficient Investing Strategies

Chapter 10 Mastering Behavioral Finance Overcoming Common Investor Biases

Chapter 11 Financial Independence and Beyond Achieving Your Dream Lifestyle

Chapter 12 Putting It All Together Your Path to Wealth

Mastery Epilogue Embracing a Lifetime of Financial Learning and Growth

CHAPTER 1
INTRODUCTION TO
FINANCIAL MASTERY

Understanding the importance of financial literacy:

Financial literacy is the foundation of financial success. It encompasses knowledge and skills related to managing money, making informed financial decisions, and achieving long-term financial goals. Without a basic understanding of financial concepts, individuals may struggle to navigate the complexities of personal finance and may be at risk of making costly mistakes. For example, someone who lacks financial literacy may not understand the implications of high-interest debt or the importance of saving for retirement, leading to financial insecurity in the long run.

Setting the foundation for financial success:

Setting the foundation for financial success involves establishing key principles and habits that support sound financial management. This includes developing a mindset of financial responsibility, setting clear financial goals, and prioritizing financial education. For instance, individuals can begin by tracking their income and expenses, creating a budget, and building an emergency fund to cover unexpected expenses. By laying this groundwork, individuals can create a solid foundation for achieving their financial aspirations.

The journey towards wealth mastery:

Wealth mastery is not simply about accumulating wealth; it's about achieving financial freedom and fulfillment. It involves mastering the principles of wealth creation, wealth preservation, and wealth distribution. The journey towards wealth mastery is a lifelong process that requires ongoing learning, adaptation, and discipline. It's about aligning your financial decisions with your values, goals, and priorities, and taking deliberate steps to build a life of abundance and purpose.

CHAPTER 2 BUILDING A STRONG FINANCIAL FOUNDATION

Assessing your current financial situation:

Assessing your current financial situation involves taking stock of your income, expenses, assets, and liabilities. This may include reviewing your bank statements, credit card statements, investment accounts, and debt obligations. By understanding your financial position, you can identify areas of strength and areas for improvement, and develop a plan to achieve your financial goals.

Setting SMART financial goals:

SMART goals are specific, measurable, achievable, relevant, and time-bound. When setting financial goals, it's important to be clear about what you want to achieve, how you will measure progress, and when you hope to accomplish them. For example, a SMART financial goal might be to save $10,000 for a down payment on a home within the next two years. By setting SMART goals, you can create a roadmap for success and stay motivated as you work towards achieving your objectives.

Creating a budget and managing expenses effectively:

A budget is a powerful tool for managing your finances and

achieving your financial goals. It involves tracking your income and expenses, categorizing your spending, and allocating your resources in a way that aligns with your priorities. By creating a budget, you can identify areas where you may be overspending and make adjustments to ensure that your money is working for you. For example, you might decide to cut back on discretionary expenses like dining out or entertainment in order to free up more money for savings or debt repayment.

CHAPTER 3 INVESTING BASICS GETTING STARTED

Demystifying the world of investing:

Investing can seem daunting, but it doesn't have to be. At its core, investing is about putting your money to work in order to generate returns over time. There are many different investment options available, including stocks, bonds, mutual funds, ETFs, real estate, and more. By understanding the basics of investing, you can make informed decisions about how to allocate your resources and build wealth over the long term.

Understanding risk and return:

Risk and return are fundamental concepts in investing. Generally, investments with higher potential returns also come with higher levels of risk. Understanding your risk tolerance – or your ability to withstand fluctuations in the value of your investments – is crucial for determining the appropriate investment strategy for your financial goals and circumstances. For example, younger investors with a longer time horizon may be more comfortable taking on greater risk in pursuit of higher returns, while older investors nearing retirement may prioritize capital preservation and income generation.

Introduction to asset classes:

Stocks, bonds, real estate, and more: Asset classes are categories of investments that share similar characteristics and risk profiles. The main asset classes include stocks (equities), bonds (fixed- income securities), real estate, and cash equivalents. Each asset class has its own unique risk and return characteristics, as well as potential benefits and drawbacks. For example, stocks offer the potential for high returns but also come with greater volatility, while bonds provide steady income and capital preservation but may offer lower returns over the long term. By diversifying across different asset classes, investors can spread risk and build a well-balanced investment portfolio.

CHAPTER 4 CRAFTING YOUR INVESTMENT STRATEGY

Determining your risk tolerance and investment timeline:

Your risk tolerance and investment timeline are two key factors that influence your investment strategy. Risk tolerance refers to your ability and willingness to withstand fluctuations in the value of your investments, while your investment timeline refers to the length of time you expect to hold your investments. By assessing your risk tolerance and investment timeline, you can tailor your investment strategy to align with your financial goals and preferences. For example, if you have a long investment horizon and a high risk tolerance, you may choose to allocate a larger portion of your portfolio to stocks, which have the potential for higher returns over the long term but also come with greater volatility.

Asset allocation strategies for optimal portfolio diversification:

Asset allocation is the process of dividing your investment portfolio among different asset classes, such as stocks, bonds, and cash equivalents. The goal of asset allocation is to achieve optimal diversification, or spreading your investments across different asset classes to reduce risk and maximize returns.

There are various asset allocation strategies to consider, including strategic asset allocation, tactical asset allocation, and dynamic asset allocation. Each strategy has its own unique approach to balancing risk and return based on market conditions, economic outlook, and investor preferences.

Selecting investment vehicles:

Mutual funds, ETFs, and individual securities: Once you have determined your asset allocation strategy, the next step is to select specific investment vehicles to implement your strategy. There are many different investment vehicles available, including mutual funds, exchange-traded funds (ETFs), and individual securities such as stocks and bonds. Each investment vehicle has its own unique features, advantages, and considerations to take into account. For example, mutual funds offer diversification and professional management but may come with higher fees, while ETFs offer low-cost access to a broad range of asset classes but may be subject to trading commissions and bid-ask spreads. By carefully evaluating your options, you can choose investment vehicles that align with your investment goals, risk tolerance, and preferences.

CHAPTER 5
MASTERING THE ART OF STOCK MARKET INVESTING

Fundamental analysis:

Evaluating stocks based on financial metrics and business fundamentals: Fundamental analysis is a method of evaluating stocks based on the underlying financial performance and business fundamentals of the companies in which you are investing. This may include analyzing financial statements, earnings reports, cash flow statements, and other key metrics to assess the health and growth potential of a company. By conducting fundamental analysis, investors can identify undervalued stocks with strong growth prospects and avoid overvalued stocks with poor fundamentals.

Technical analysis:

Analyzing price charts and market trends: Technical analysis is a method of evaluating stocks based on historical price charts and market trends. This may involve analyzing price patterns, chart patterns, volume trends, and other technical indicators to identify potential buying and selling opportunities. While fundamental analysis focuses on the intrinsic value of a company, technical analysis focuses on the supply and demand dynamics of the market and investor sentiment. By incorporating technical analysis into your investment approach, you can gain insights into short-term price movements and identify potential entry and exit points for your trades.

Common stock market myths and misconceptions:

There are many myths and misconceptions surrounding the stock market and investing that can lead to poor decision-making and missed opportunities. For example, one common myth is that investing in the stock market is akin to gambling, when in fact, investing involves careful analysis and disciplined decision-making. Another myth is that you need a large amount of money to start investing, when in reality, you can begin investing with as little as a few hundred dollars. By dispelling these myths and educating yourself about the realities of investing, you can make more informed decisions and avoid common pitfalls in the stock market.

CHAPTER 6
NAVIGATING THE BOND MARKET AND FIXED-INCOME INVESTMENTS

Understanding bonds and fixed-income securities:

Bonds are fixed-income securities that represent loans made by investors to governments, corporations, or other entities. When you invest in a bond, you are essentially lending money to the issuer in exchange for regular interest payments and the return of the principal amount at maturity. Bonds come in various types and structures, including government bonds, corporate bonds, municipal bonds, and Treasury bonds. Each type of bond has its own unique features, credit risks, and potential returns. By understanding the basics of bonds and fixed- income securities, investors can diversify their portfolios and manage risk more effectively.

Types of bonds:

Government bonds, corporate bonds, municipal bonds, and more: Government bonds are issued by national governments and are considered to be among the safest investments available, as they are backed by the full faith and credit of the issuing government. Corporate bonds are issued by corporations to raise capital for various purposes, such as funding expansion projects or refinancing debt. Municipal bonds are issued by state and local governments to finance public projects, such as schools, roads, and infrastructure. Treasury bonds are issued by the U.S. Department of the Treasury and are considered to be risk-free investments, as they are backed by the U.S. government. Each type of bond has its own unique risk profile, yield characteristics, and tax implications, making it important for investors to carefully evaluate their options and diversify their bond holdings accordingly.

Yield curve analysis and interest rate risk management:

The yield curve is a graphical representation of the relationship between the yields (interest rates) and maturities of bonds of the same credit quality. By analyzing the shape of the yield curve, investors can gain insights into future economic conditions and interest rate expectations. For example, a steeply upward-sloping yield curve may indicate expectations of strong economic growth and rising inflation, while an inverted yield curve may signal expectations of economic recession and falling interest rates. Understanding the yield curve and interest rate risk is crucial for managing bond portfolios and adjusting investment strategies accordingly.

CHAPTER 7 REAL ESTATE INVESTING GENERATING PASSIVE INCOME AND BUILDING WEALTH

Introduction to real estate investing:

Rental properties, REITs, and real estate crowdfunding: Real estate investing involves purchasing, owning, and managing properties for the purpose of generating rental income, capital appreciation, or both. There are various ways to invest in real estate, including direct ownership of rental properties, investing in real estate investment trusts (REITs), and participating in real estate crowdfunding platforms. Each investment option has its own unique advantages and considerations to take into account. For example, direct ownership of rental properties offers the potential for high returns and control over investment decisions but requires active management and carries risks such as vacancy and maintenance costs. REITs, on the other hand, provide passive exposure to real estate markets and offer liquidity and diversification benefits but may be subject to market volatility and management fees. Real estate crowdfunding platforms allow investors to pool their capital to invest in specific real estate projects or properties, offering access to opportunities that may be otherwise out of reach for individual investors.

Evaluating real estate opportunities:

Location, cash flow, and appreciation potential: When evaluating real estate opportunities, investors should consider a variety of factors, including the location of the property, its potential for rental income and cash flow, and its appreciation potential over time. Location is often cited as one of the most important factors in real estate investing, as properties in desirable areas tend to command higher rents and experience greater appreciation. Cash flow, or the income generated by the property after expenses, is another key consideration, as positive cash flow can provide a steady stream of income and help cover expenses such as mortgage payments, property taxes, and maintenance costs. Finally, investors should assess the appreciation potential of the property, taking into account factors such as local market trends, economic conditions, and development activity. By conducting thorough due diligence and analyzing these factors, investors can identify real estate opportunities that align with their investment objectives and risk tolerance.

Financing options and strategies for real estate investments:

Financing is an important aspect of real estate investing, as it can impact the affordability, profitability, and risk profile of an investment. There are various financing options available to real estate investors, including conventional mortgages, government-backed loans, and alternative financing sources such as private lenders and hard money lenders. Each financing option has its own eligibility requirements, terms, and costs, so it's important for investors to compare their options and choose the financing solution that best meets their needs. In addition to selecting the right financing option, investors should also consider strategies for leveraging their investment capital and maximizing returns. For example, using leverage, or borrowing money to finance a portion of the purchase price, can amplify returns and increase cash- on-cash returns, but it also increases the risk of financial loss in the event of market downturns or adverse economic conditions. By carefully evaluating financing options and implementing sound investment strategies, real estate investors can build wealth and achieve their financial goals over time.

CHAPTER 8
RETIREMENT PLANNING AND WEALTH PRESERVATION

The importance of retirement planning and saving for the future: Retirement planning is a critical aspect of financial planning, as it involves preparing for your financial needs and goals in retirement. Whether you're decades away from retirement or nearing retirement age, it's never too early or too late to start saving and planning for your future. Retirement planning involves estimating your future expenses, determining your retirement income needs, and identifying strategies to accumulate savings and assets to support your desired lifestyle in retirement. By starting early and making regular contributions to retirement accounts such as 401(k) plans, IRAs, and Roth IRAs, you can take advantage of compounding returns and maximize your retirement savings over time.

Retirement account options: 401(k), IRA, Roth IRA, and pension plans: There are various retirement account options available to individuals and families, each with its own unique features, tax advantages, and eligibility requirements. Employer-sponsored retirement plans, such as 401(k) plans, are a common way to save for retirement, offering tax-deferred contributions, employer matching contributions, and a wide range of investment options. Individual retirement accounts (IRAs) are another popular retirement savings vehicle, providing tax-advantaged savings options for individuals who do not have access to an employer-sponsored plan or who want to supplement their workplace retirement savings. Roth IRAs offer tax-free withdrawals in retirement but are subject to income eligibility limits and contribution limits. Pension plans, which are increasingly rare in the private sector, provide guaranteed retirement income for eligible employees based on years of service and salary history. By understanding the features and benefits of different retirement account options, you can choose the right mix of accounts to achieve your retirement goals and optimize your tax situation.

Estate planning:

Wills, trusts, and legacy planning: Estate planning is an essential component of retirement planning and wealth preservation, as it involves making arrangements for the management and distribution of your assets and affairs after your death. A comprehensive estate plan typically includes a will, which outlines your wishes for the distribution of your assets and the care of minor children, and may also include trusts, powers of attorney, advance directives, and other legal documents to address specific needs and concerns. Estate planning is not just for the wealthy – it's for anyone who wants to ensure that their wishes are carried out and their loved ones are provided for after they're gone. By working with an experienced estate planning attorney, you can create a customized estate plan that reflects your values, priorities, and goals, and provides peace of mind for you and your family.

CHAPTER 9 TAX-EFFICIENT INVESTING STRATEGIES

Understanding the impact of taxes on investment returns:

Taxes can have a significant impact on investment returns, so it's important to understand how different types of investments are taxed and to implement tax-efficient investment strategies. For example, income from investments such as interest, dividends, and capital gains may be subject to federal income tax, state income tax, and capital gains tax, depending on the type of account in which the investments are held and the investor's tax bracket. By minimizing taxes on investment income and optimizing tax deductions and credits, investors can enhance their after-tax returns and keep more of their money working for them.

Tax-efficient investment vehicles and strategies:

There are various tax-efficient investment vehicles and strategies available to investors, each with its own unique tax advantages and considerations. For example, retirement accounts such as 401(k) plans, IRAs, and Roth IRAs offer tax-deferred or tax-free growth, allowing investments to compound without being subject to current income tax. Taxable brokerage accounts may offer greater flexibility and liquidity but are subject to taxes on investment income and capital gains. Tax- loss harvesting is a strategy that involves selling investments at a loss to offset capital gains and reduce tax liability. Municipal bonds, which are issued by state and local governments, may offer tax-free income for investors in high tax brackets. By incorporating tax-efficient investment vehicles and strategies into your overall investment plan, you can minimize taxes and maximize after-tax returns over the long term.

Maximizing tax deductions and credits for long-term wealth accumulation: In addition to optimizing investment returns, investors can also take advantage of various tax deductions and credits to reduce their overall tax burden and increase their disposable income. Common tax deductions and credits include deductions for retirement contributions, such as contributions to 401(k) plans, IRAs, and Health Savings Accounts (HSAs), which can reduce taxable income and lower tax liability. Other deductions may include mortgage interest, property taxes, charitable contributions, and medical expenses. Tax credits, such as the Earned Income Tax Credit (EITC) and the

Child Tax Credit, provide direct reductions in tax liability for eligible taxpayers. By understanding the tax code and leveraging available deductions and credits, investors can keep more of their hard-earned money and accelerate their progress towards their financial goals.

CHAPTER 10
MASTERING BEHAVIORAL FINANCE OVERCOMING COMMON INVESTOR BIASES

Understanding investor psychology and behavioral biases:

Behavioral finance is a field of study that examines how psychological factors and cognitive biases influence investor behavior and decision-making. Common investor biases include overconfidence, confirmation bias, loss aversion, and herd mentality, among others. These biases can lead investors to make irrational decisions, such as buying high and selling low, chasing performance, or ignoring important information. By understanding the underlying psychological drivers of investor behavior, individuals can recognize their own biases and develop strategies to overcome them.

Techniques for overcoming common investing pitfalls:

There are various techniques and strategies that investors can use to overcome common investing pitfalls and improve their decision-making. For example, setting clear investment goals and maintaining a long- term perspective can help investors stay focused on their objectives and resist the temptation to react impulsively to short-term market fluctuations. Diversification, or spreading investments across different asset classes and sectors, can help reduce risk and minimize the impact of individual investment losses. Dollar-cost averaging is a strategy that involves investing a fixed amount of money at regular intervals, regardless of market conditions, which can help smooth out market volatility and potentially lower the average cost of investments over time. By incorporating these and other techniques into their investment approach, investors can mitigate the impact of behavioral biases and make more rational and disciplined decisions.

Building emotional resilience and discipline in investing:

Emotional resilience and discipline are essential qualities for successful investing, as they enable investors to stay focused on their long-term goals and maintain composure in the face of market volatility and uncertainty. Building emotional resilience involves developing self-awareness, mindfulness, and emotional intelligence, as well as cultivating positive coping mechanisms and stress management techniques. Discipline, on the other hand, involves sticking to a well-thought-out investment plan, avoiding impulsive decisions, and resisting the urge to chase short-term market trends. By cultivating these qualities and practicing disciplined investing habits, investors can navigate market fluctuations with confidence and achieve greater success over the long term.

CHAPTER 11 FINANCIAL INDEPENDENCE AND BEYOND ACHIEVING YOUR DREAM LIFESTYLE

The concept of financial independence and early retirement:

Financial independence is the ability to cover your living expenses and achieve your desired lifestyle without the need to actively work for income. Achieving financial independence allows individuals to pursue their passions, interests, and dreams on their own terms, without being constrained by financial obligations or employment commitments. Early retirement, or FIRE (Financial Independence, Retire Early), is a movement that advocates for achieving financial independence at a young age, often in one's 30s or 40s, through frugal living, aggressive saving, and strategic investing. By achieving financial independence and early retirement, individuals can gain greater freedom, flexibility, and autonomy in how they spend their time and resources.

Creating multiple streams of passive income:

Passive income is income generated from sources other than active employment, such as rental income, dividends, interest, royalties, and business income. Creating multiple streams of passive income is a key strategy for achieving financial independence and building wealth over time. By diversifying sources of income and leveraging assets to generate passive cash flow, individuals can reduce reliance on earned income and create financial resilience. Examples of passive income streams include rental properties, dividend-paying stocks, peer-to-peer lending, affiliate marketing, and online courses. By building a portfolio of passive income streams, individuals can create a stable and sustainable source of income that supports their financial goals and aspirations.

Designing your dream lifestyle and legacy:

Designing your dream lifestyle involves envisioning the life you want to live and taking deliberate steps to make it a reality. This may include setting personal and professional goals, prioritizing activities and experiences that bring you joy and fulfillment, and aligning your lifestyle choices with your values and priorities. Legacy planning involves thinking about the impact you want to leave on the world and planning for how you want to be remembered after you're gone. This may include creating a charitable foundation, endowing a scholarship fund, or passing down values, traditions, and assets to future generations. By designing your dream lifestyle and legacy, you can create a life of purpose, meaning, and significance that reflects your unique talents, passions, and contributions.

CHAPTER 12 PUTTING IT ALL TOGETHER YOUR PATH TO WEALTH MASTERY

Reviewing key concepts and strategies for financial success:

In this final chapter, we review key concepts and strategies covered throughout the book and reflect on the journey towards wealth mastery. From building a strong financial foundation to mastering the art of investing, retirement planning, and achieving financial independence, we've explored the fundamental principles and practical techniques for achieving financial success. By putting these concepts into practice and taking consistent action towards your goals, you can chart a course towards a future of abundance, security, and fulfillment.

Creating a personalized financial plan and roadmap:

Building wealth and achieving financial mastery requires a personalized approach that reflects your unique circumstances, goals, and values. In this chapter, we discuss how to create a personalized financial plan and roadmap that aligns with your aspirations and guides your decision-making. This may involve assessing your current financial situation, setting SMART financial goals, and identifying strategies and tactics to achieve them. By developing a clear plan of action and staying committed to your goals, you can navigate the complexities of personal finance with confidence and clarity.

Taking action towards achieving your financial goals:

Ultimately, the key to wealth mastery is taking action. In this chapter, we discuss strategies for overcoming common obstacles and barriers to action, such as procrastination, fear of failure, and self-doubt. We explore techniques for building momentum, staying motivated, and maintaining accountability as you work towards your financial goals. Whether it's setting up automatic savings contributions, starting an investment portfolio, or launching a side hustle, taking consistent action is the foundation of financial success. By embracing a mindset of continuous improvement and learning, you can transform your financial future and create a life of abundance and prosperity.

EPILOGUE EMBRACING A LIFETIME OF FINANCIAL LEARNING AND GROWTH

The journey towards wealth mastery is ongoing: In this final section, we reflect on the idea that the journey towards wealth mastery is ongoing and ever-evolving. Financial success is not a destination to be reached, but a journey to be embraced and enjoyed. As we continue to learn, grow, and adapt to changing circumstances and opportunities, we expand our capacity for abundance, resilience, and impact. Whether you're just starting out on your financial journey or you've been on the path for years, there is always more to learn, explore, and experience. By embracing the journey and staying open to new possibilities, we can create lives of purpose, fulfillment, and joy.

Cultivating a mindset of continuous learning and adaptation: In the world of personal finance, knowledge is power. In this epilogue, we emphasize the importance of cultivating a mindset of continuous learning and adaptation as we navigate the complexities of financial life. By staying curious, seeking out new information, and being open to new ideas and perspectives, we can expand our horizons, sharpen our skills, and make better decisions for ourselves and our loved ones. Whether it's reading books and articles, attending seminars and workshops, or engaging with a community of like-minded individuals, there are countless opportunities to deepen our understanding of personal finance and improve our financial well-being.

Empowering others to achieve financial success and abundance: As we conclude our journey towards wealth mastery, we recognize the importance of paying it forward and empowering others to achieve financial success and abundance. In this epilogue, we discuss strategies for sharing our knowledge, experiences, and resources with others, whether it's through mentoring, coaching, volunteering, or philanthropy. By lifting others up and helping them overcome obstacles and barriers to financial success, we create a ripple effect of positive change that extends far beyond ourselves. Together, we can build a world where everyone has the opportunity to thrive and prosper, regardless of their background or circumstances.

APPENDIX

Resources for Further Learning and Action

Recommended books, websites, and podcasts for financial education: In this appendix, we provide a curated list of recommended books, websites, and podcasts for further learning and action in the realm of personal finance. These resources cover a wide range of topics, including budgeting, investing, retirement planning, tax strategies, and behavioral finance, and are designed to help you deepen your understanding of key concepts and take practical steps towards achieving your financial goals. Whether you're looking for beginner-friendly guides, advanced strategies, or inspiring stories of financial success, there's something for everyone on this list.

Tools and calculators for financial planning and analysis: In this section, we highlight tools and calculators that can help you plan and analyze your finances more effectively. These tools cover a variety of financial planning needs, including budgeting, debt repayment, retirement planning, investment analysis, and tax estimation. Whether you're creating a budget, evaluating investment opportunities, or projecting your retirement income needs, these tools can provide valuable insights and help you make informed decisions about your financial future.

Professional organizations and networks for financial professionals and enthusiasts: Finally, we provide a list of professional organizations and networks for financial professionals and enthusiasts. These organizations offer opportunities for networking, continuing education, certification, and professional development in the field of personal finance. Whether you're a financial advisor, accountant, planner, analyst, or simply a passionate advocate for financial literacy, joining a professional organization can help you connect with peers, stay current on industry trends, and advance your career or personal interests in finance. From local chapters and meetups to national conferences and online forums, there are many ways to get involved and make a difference in the world of personal finance.

www.ingramcontent.com/pod-product-compliance
Lightning Source LLC
Chambersburg PA
CBHW050249230526
45470CB00005B/2180